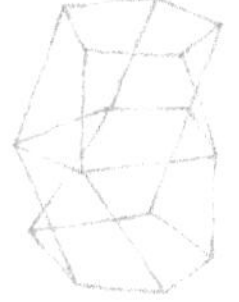

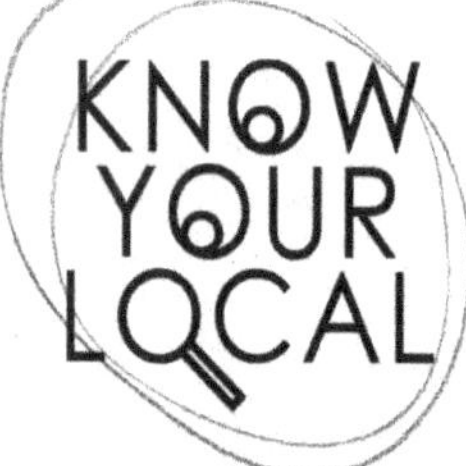

Buckman Publishing LLC
est. 2018
1448 NE 28th Ave
Portland, Oregon 97232
buckmanjournal.com

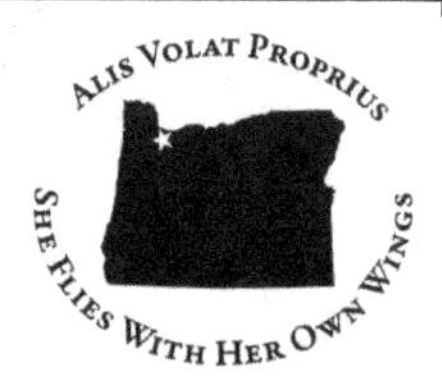

Congratulations! A Buckman production is in your hands! We're an unorthodox operation that continues the daredevil tradition of literature, printing new sparks that ignite imagination. Proudly independent, Buckman's defiant attitude aims to inspire and increase readership in greater society.

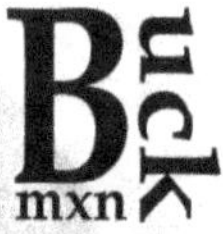

Buckman operates from our home in the upper left of Turtle Island at the confluence of the Whilamut and Wimahl rivers, among the waters and lands of the Cayuse, Clackamas, Multnomah, St'pulmsh (Cowlitz) Umatilla, Walla Walla, and Watlala peoples.

TINY HAIKU

COLLECTED WORKS FROM 2014 - 2017

POEMS BY DANIEL O'BRIEN-BRAVI

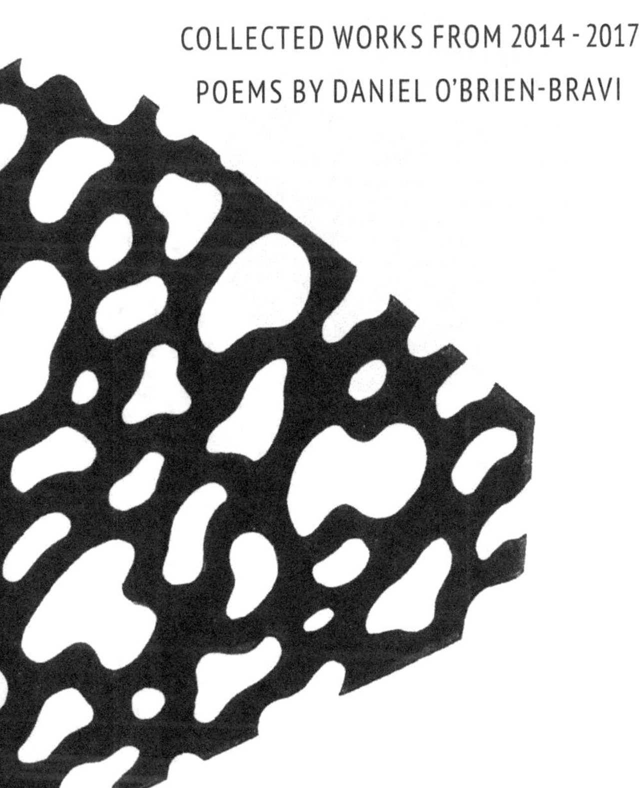

as the season turns
days retreat earlier and
yet it is timely.

10.27.14

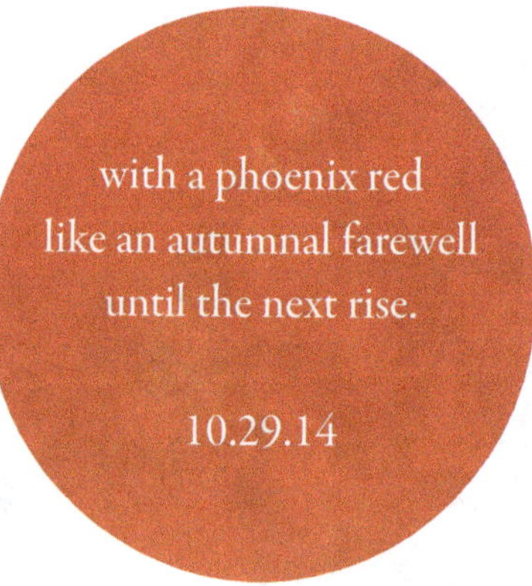

don't stop believin'
but scientific method
wasn't journey's thing.

11.07.14

pumpkin spice latte
is also cinderella's
hip hop pseudonym.

11.09.14

baristas be like
"that's a mean tamper you got"
tryin' to make puns.

11.16.14

let's get real, ice-t
it's weird to write "cop killer"
then do s.v.u.

11.19.14

like ghost orchid blooms
behold the rare beauty of
portland's umbrellas.

11.23.14

these boots are made for
looking good while unlaced and
that's just what they'll do.

11.23.14

christopher walken
runs into a bar & says
"this might be wordplay!"

12.10.14

I SAID "SWEET AS SUGAR"
AS A COMPLIMENT BECAUSE
I'M NOT A DENTIST.
[OR]
MY DENTIST IS SLY
HE SAID "YOU'RE SWEET AS SUGAR"
WHICH MEANT I'M TROUBLE.

12.16.14

I can't escape you
or it might just be other
car2go rentals.

12.17.14

I have a theory
that dentists prefer when you
use only vowels.

12.22.14

sharing your presence
can be as rewarding as
giving some presents.

12.26.14

year of the dragon!
wait, is it the year of the
oh look free champagne!

12.31.14

THERE'S SOMETHING ABOUT
VAGUE PONDERINGS THAT MAKE ME
WATCH NETFLIX INSTEAD.
[OR]
WHAT WAS I SAYING?

01.12.15

POLYSYLLABIC
QUASI-INTELLECTUAL
MANIFESTATION.

01.07.15

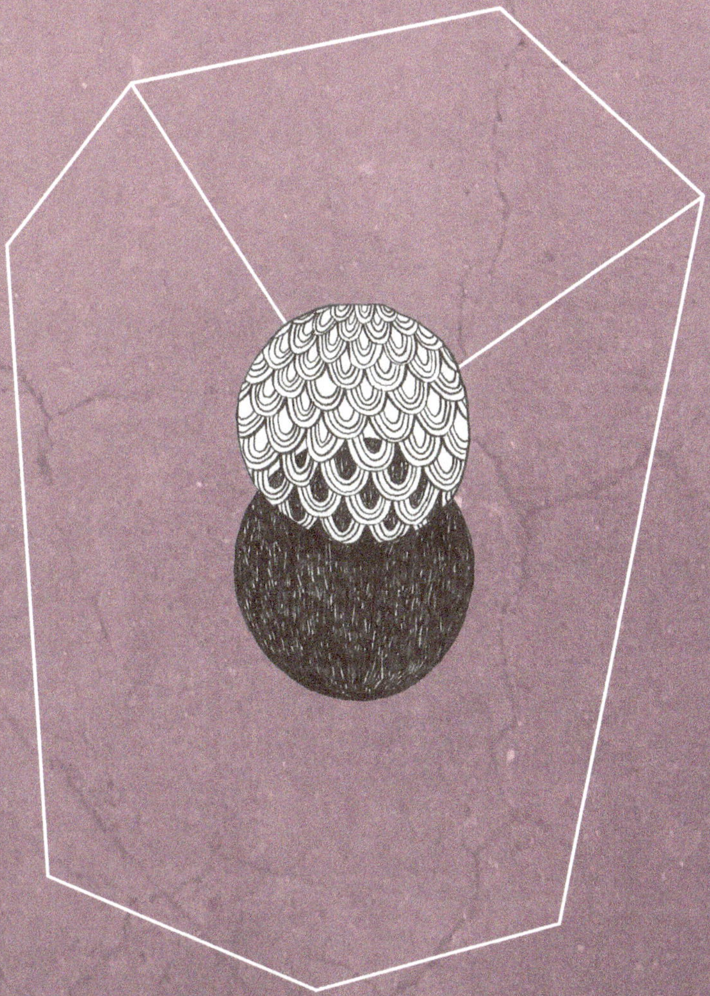

hunter-gatherers
convene at fred meyer to
stalk veggie hot dogs.

01.12.15

rock paper scissors
is too honest about a
fist smashing peace signs.

01.21.15

forrest gump was wrong
because chocolate boxes
are clearly labeled.

02.04.15

roses smell so good
that everything should smell
wait no that's crazy.

02.04.15

congratulations!
you've been selected to mark
this email as spam.

02.11.15

I can either sleep
or the internet and I
can beat this dead horse.

02.18.15

you drop down ch'bahhh
you hit the lip like w'pah!
pitted, so pitted.

03.12.15

mr. pibb is proof
that dr. pepper wasted
money on degrees.

03.18.15

if you repeat the
word "buffalo" eight times it's
a complete sentence.

03.18.15

read rhymes with red but
read doesn't rhyme with read, so
thanks for that, english.

03.25.15

"don't fear the reaper"
is definitely not what
a farmer would say.

03.30.15

house music is like
bass snare bass snare bass snare bass
repeat for effect.

03.30.15

telecommuting
on information highways
really megabytes.

04.22.15

HAIKUS NEED NOT RHYME
BUT INSPIRATION KNOWS NO
CERTAIN PLACE OR TIME.
[OR]
HAIKUS NEED NOT RHYME
BUT IT DOES MAKE FOR A GOOD
WAY TO WASTE SOME TIME.

05.06.15

if you think about
it enough, endings really
only matter if.

05.13.15

when the going gets
tough, basic logic tells you
going solves nothing.

05.28.15

all I'm saying is
fade-outs on records should be
replicated live.

06.02.15
#wheresthelie

you know it's summer
when you hit that slip-n-slide
so hard you forget.

06.17.15

speed bumps & potholes
combine to create problems
quite sisyphean.

06.24.15

it's so frickin' hot
it's so hot sweet lord jesus
kill me kill me now.

07.01.15
#tracy

LIFE IS LIKE A BOX
OF CHOCOLATES, YOU NEVER
-LEAVE IT IN THE SUN.
-PREFER IT MELTED.

do a little dance
make a little love and get
acquainted later.

07.04.15

HYPERBOLE IS
THE BEST THING FOREVER AND
EVER AND EVER.
[OR]
HYPERBOLE IS
LITERALLY THE BEST THING
TO EVER EXIST.

07.06.15

I'M REALLY REALLY
SORRY FOR DROPPING THE BALL
ON HAIKUS LATELY.
[OR]
I HOPE THIS HAIKU
WAS WORTH THE WAIT, SO FAR
I DON'T THINK IT WAS.
[OR]
PERSONALLY I
DON'T THINK THIS HAIKU WAS WORTH
WAITING TWO WHOLE WEEKS.

07.29.15

if you don't cover
pie with ice cream, that's okay
but we are not friends.

08.06.15

complaining about
rent in portland is better
as performance art.

08.07.15

ever wonder who
what where when why how could
should do did does will?

08.07.15

remember that time
I sounded like a stoner
yeah me neither man.

08.07.15

let's make a wager
that you'll be gambling by the
end of this haiku.

08.12.15

talking about rent
in portland is best done by
performance artists.

08.17.15

talking about rent
in portland is now a form
of performancc art.

08.17.15

talking about ~~rent~~ smoke
in portland is now a form
of performance art.

08.~~17~~23.15

how many other
bodily functions can we
say "god bless you" for?

08.26.15

I don't want no scrubs
scrubs are an outfit that say
"please get blood on me."

08.26.15

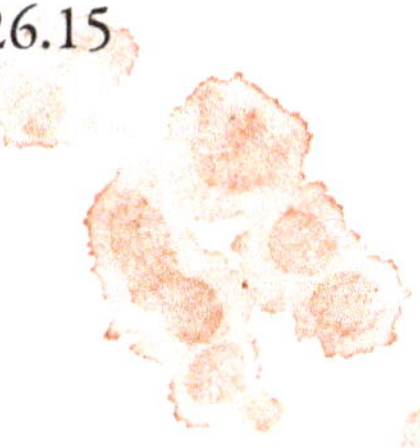

abraham lincoln
once said "I've never seen such
a respectful and -"

08.31.15

I like to think that
'trickle down economics'
fails on name alone.

08.31.15

9.2 PORTLAND HAIKU STUFF
- Good stuff ~~FADING~~ AWAY
- AFFORDABILITY
- DEVELOPMENT
- HOMELESS
- LIBERAL - XENOPHOBIC

EXCUSE ME, BUT IF
YOU'RE DONE WITH YOUR CULTURE, I
~~xxxxxxxxxxxxxxxx~~ HAVE CONDOS TO BUILD.

PORTLAND: FOR FANS OF
LIBERAL XENOPHOBES WHO
LOVE CONTRADICTIONS

IF SAN FRANCISCO
ABORTED ITS BABY WITH
WYOMING: PORTLAND

IF POLITICAL   (BUT NOT REALLY)
CORRECTNESS ~~xxxx~~ AND BEING SMUG
GETS YOU OFF: PORTLAND

DONUTS, PIZZA, ~~xxxx~~ BEER,
~~xxx~~ COFFEE, BIKES AND STRIPPERS ARE
OUR ~~xxxxxxx~~ ICE CREAM FLAVORS

DONUTS, PIZZA, BEER,
COFFEE, BIKES, AND STRIPPERS ALL
FIT UNDER CONDOS.

OUR NEWEST ICE CREAM
FLAVOR PAIRS DISPLACEMENT WITH
GENTRIFICATION.

09.02.15

mustaches are a
good way to say "I'm lazy,
but maybe handsome?"

09.02.15

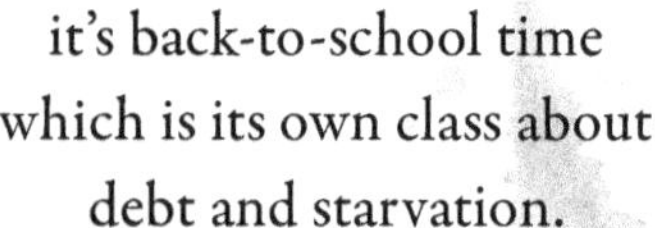

it's back-to-school time
which is its own class about
debt and starvation.

09.09.15

watching butterflies
and seeing how butter flies
are quite different.

09.22.15

catching butterflies
involves a different net
than flying butter.

09.22.15

FEAR OF THE UNKNOWN
IS COMMON, BUT FEAR OF THE
DARK IS CHILDISH.
[OR]
FEARING THE UNKNOWN
IS COMMON, BUT FEARING THE
DARK IS MOCKED SOMEHOW.
[OR]
FEAR OF THE DARK IS
FEARING THE UNKNOWN SIMPLY
DISMISSED AS CHILDISH.

10.14.15

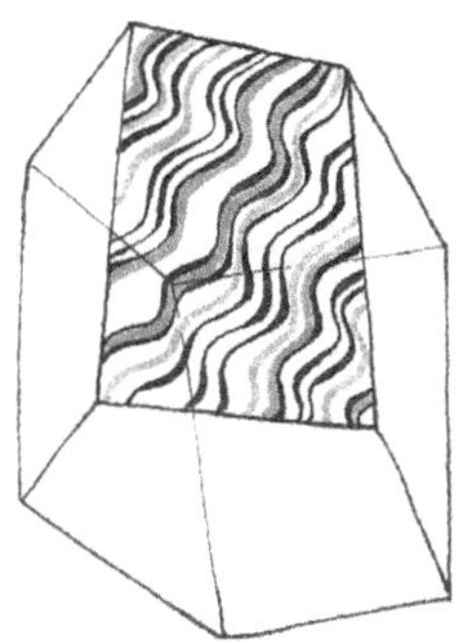

- AT THIS TIME LAST YEAR
- IT'S BEEN ONE YEAR SINCE
- STARTED "TINY HAIKU"
- AND THE NEXT YEAR WILL —
- THANKS FOR ALL THE MEM.
- AND IT'S BEEN REALLY —

10-28

it's that time of year
when friends get together and
loathe christmas music.

11.04.15

thou shall not purchase
boring white socks as a gift.
santa 3:18.

11.04.15

FUN FACT: "BLACK FRIDAY"
ORIGINATED IN THE
VOID WHERE "LOVE" ONCE WAS.
[OR]
FUN FACT: "BLACK FRIDAY"
IS EVERY DAY IN THE
MARIANA TRENCH.
[OR]
FUN FACT: "BLACK FRIDAY"
IS THE ONLY DAY IN THE
MARIANA TRENCH.

11.25.15

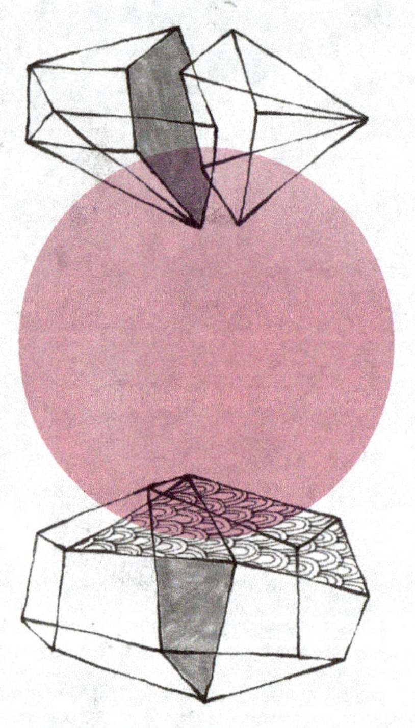

PALINDROME HAIKUS

MADAM'S DOG SEES GOD
AS A REVIVER, AS A
DOG SEES GOD'S MADAM

SIRI'S DOG SEES GOD
AS A REVIVER, AS A
DOG SEES GOD'S IRIS

SAGAS: DOG SEES GOD
AS A REVIVER, AS A
DOG SEES GOD'S A GAS.

DAD'S DOG SEES GOD
AS A LIVE EVIL, AS A
DOG SEES GOD'S DAD
11·21

the safest version
of the u.s. isn't the
one covered in guns.

12.03.15
#patriot

comparing apples
to oranges? why not try
apples to pickles?

12.09.15

if rules are made to
be broken, then my only
rule is: break all rules.

12.09.15

happy holidays!
to be specific, the day
of brumalia.

12.09.15

"happy holidays"
is almost as offensive
as "happy near year."

12.09.15

only three-hundred
and sixty-six days til next
christmas! can't wait!

12.24.15

for twenty years
I've been true to "no more new
year's resolutions."

12.26.15

define "militia"
because it's not likely a
bunch of angry dudes.

01.04.16

black men are thugs and
muslims are terrorists and
white men labeled them.

01.04.16

I miss the days of
old calendars inciting
apocalypse fears.

01.06.16

remember to give
strength to the common man, they
are the foundation.

01.11.16

if the lowest class
is the foundation, why should
it be the weakest?

01.11.16

the only problem
with predictable haikus
is here's the plot twist.

01.21.16

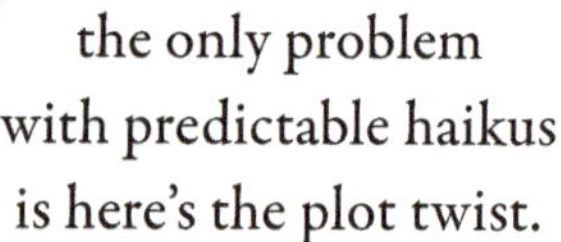

I just want a prez
that's all like "yo yo yo yo
pizza is so good."

01.21.16

yes we have wifi.
yes it's local, free range, &
super organic.

01.21.16

I'm at an art show
when I overhear "I'd put
that piece on my fridge."

01.21.16

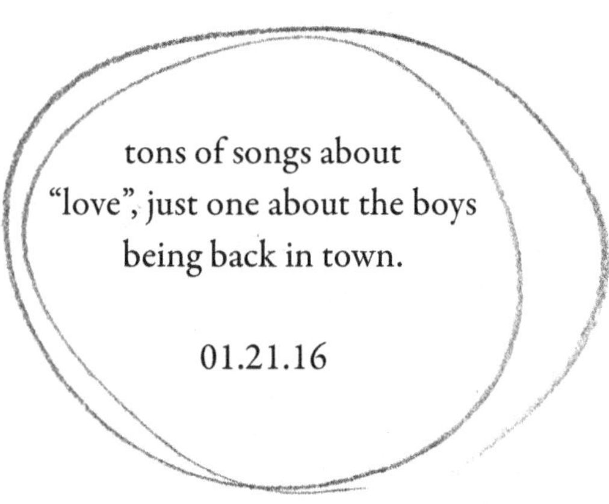

sadly, bernie has
<u>no stance</u> on what he would do
for a klondike bar.

01.27.16

#tinyhaiku
#feelthefreezerbern
#WWBD

the best valentine's
present is not electing
trump as president.

02.04.16

HAVE YOU HEARD THAT JOKE
ABOUT BUDGETING FOR WARS
& OIL BUT NOT ROADS?
[OR]
BUDGET TALK: WARS FOR
OIL FOR CARS: BILLIONS! BRIDGES
AND ROADS FOR CARS - MEH.
[OR]
BAIL OUT THE AUTO
INDUSTRY WHILE BRIDGES AND
ROADS FALL APART: NOPE.

02.17.16

Tiny

MAKE AME:
GREAT AG
CA GREAT

2-

Haiku

I CA
N MAKEAMERI
GAIN MAKE

STMYMIND

[MUSKRAT]

IN DEAD WINTERS, ELK
ARE KNOWN TO EAT A MUSKRAT'S
HOME INSTEAD OF IT.

ELK WOULD RATHER EAT
THE HOME OF A MUSKRAT THAN
THE MUSKRAT ITSELF.

STARVING ELK WILL EAT
A MUSKRAT'S HOME, BUT NOT THE
ANIMAL ITSELF.

03.07.16

hark! what tragedy
oh, where for art thou daniel?
haikus unwritten.

03.02.16
#undernewmgmt

I, so old, can't greet
death's fatally unmoving
animosity.

03.22.16

what an amazing
week to sunbathe & read up
on global warming.

03.22.16
#whatbeautifulweatherwehavecreated
#blessed

pour some sugar on
tea, ooh, get that sucrose love
it's cold, icy sweet.

04.28.16

the bumper stickers
are abundant, but portland
is no longer weird.

04.28.16

rent skyrockets, they
camp under bridges, at least
portland is kept weird.

04.28.16
#campportlandweird

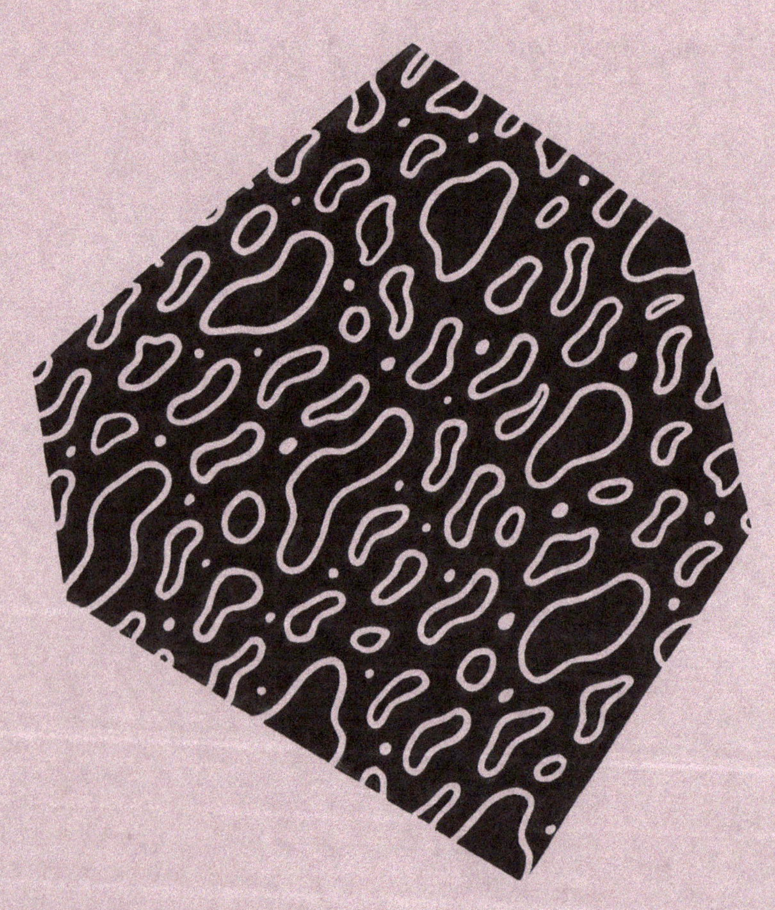

II
the boys are back, where,
you ask? why, in town, of course
they are <u>back</u> indeed

III
I remember a
time when the boys were absent
we sang about love

IV
now we can sing a
most glorious song, one with
<u>dual</u> <u>guitar</u> <u>leads</u>.

05.03.16

V

for just one moment
let's suppose the boys are,
sadly, out of town

VI

dare I suggest
"boy-less town" rhymes with "joy-less
frown" for a reason?

VII

fret not, listeners
for I have uncovered a
golden egg of hope

VIII

citizens with frowns
turn them upside-down, for the
boys are back in town.

05.12.16

IX

okay okay hear
me out - if the boys really
<u>are</u> back, then hurray!

X

but if this is all
some type of government hoax
then we must act now

XI

arise, citizens!
take to the streets and let your
voices swell like waves

XII

sing! sing a song that
proliferates the return
of the boys to town!

05.23.16

XIII

I think we can all
agree that the town is complete
with the boys' return

XIV

let's not soon forget
how their absence affected
small mom-n-pop stores

XV

sure we wrote awesome
songs when the location of
"the boys" was "in town"

XVI
without the boys in
town, the customer base has
less buying power

XVII
this means less income
which means less growth which means jobs
will soon disappear

XVIII
the truth is that one
cannot exist without the
other, so to speak.

06.02.16

BOOKS: DON'T JUDGE THEM BY
THEIR COVER. CLEARANCE DUVET
-SETS: JUDGE THEM HARSHLY.
-COVERS YOU SHOULD JUDGE.

06.07.16
#TINYHAIKU
#RUNFORBEDCOVER
#YOUARENTFOOLINGANYONEIKEA

remember that song
"wonderwall" by oasis?
what a nightmare yuck.

06.16.16

a person of grate
persuasion altered how we
eat parmesan cheese.

06.20.16

repressing buttons
& repressing feelings are
very different.

06.21.16

hot dogs & beer &
more gun deaths than anywhere
yay, independence!

07.04.16
#wheresthelie

"TAXATION WITHOUT
REPRESENTATION" IS A
BIGGER PROBLEM NOW

WHICH MAKES ME WONDER
IF PEOPLE ARE THE PROBLEM
NOT "THE GOVERNMENT"
7.4

my heart aches for the
first person who said "maybe
<u>sad</u> clowns are funny."

07.13.16

okay... [nervous laugh]
this "trump" thing has gone way way
way way way too far.

07.26.16

daniel writes haiku
one thousand monkeys typing
worked out how we thought.

08.03.16
#haikubomb
[maggie & adam]

haikubomb shmaiku
shmomb, who was "shakespeare" on the
planet of the apes?

08.04.16
#haikubattle

mother of seitan
red mill's profit of protein
gluten our savior.

#haikubomb
[maggie]

gluten vegan trap
hail vile seitan turducken
the feast you can't eat.

#haikubomb
[allen]

IF "ABSENCE MAKES THE
HEART GROW FONDER", THEN MY LOVE
GROWS WHILE YOU'RE AWAY.

IF "OUT OF SIGHT" IS
"OUT OF MIND" THEN MY LOVE WANES
DURING YOUR ABSENCE.

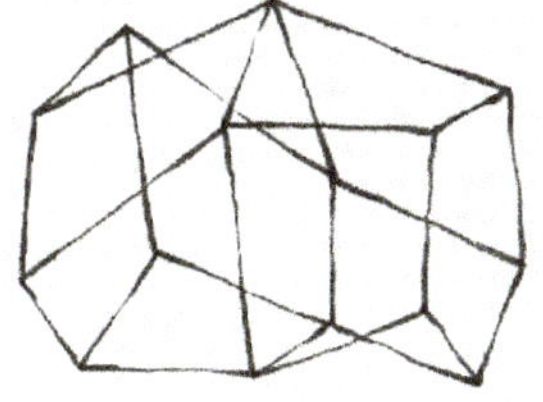

IF I SUBSCRIBE TO
EITHER, THEN MY LOVE IS FOR
RATIONALIZING.

when there's something strange...
in your neighborhood... who ya
think tweeted it first.

08.08.16

dig a pony boy
george michael j. fox in the
henhouse of card tricks.

08.15.16

rock paper scissors
10,000 b.c. version
unbeatable rock.

09.01.16

there will never be
one road for you love mountains
and I, the seasons.

09.19.16

tiny's will gladly host
support groups for victims
of this election.

11.09.16

20-17

as prime numbers go, it's a
little "on the nose."

purge this darkness through
projection, fore rampant itt
ruins for cellar stead
1.2

finished.

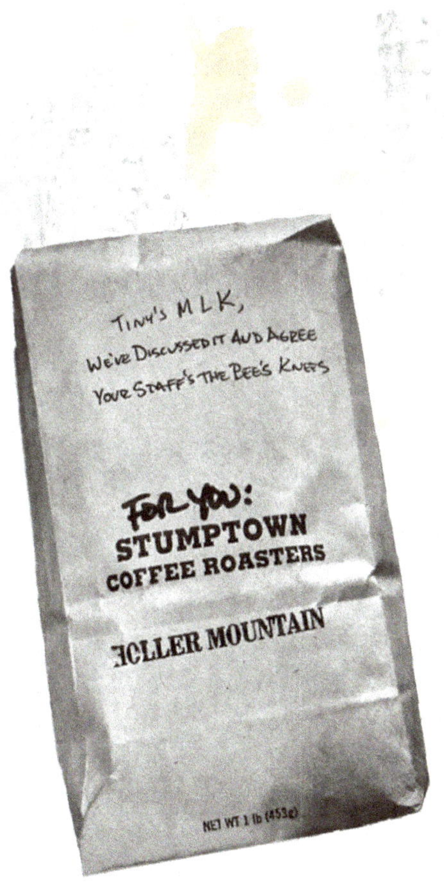

For the Tiny's Coffee community, friends, and haiku-lovers
abound. Thank you all for the ideas and support, we think
you're the bee's knees too.

<3

Daniel Robert Ubald Ferrarini O'Brien-Bravi was born on July 18th, which is the date that the great fire of Rome began. He was born a Bravi, made himself an O'Brien, discovered he was never either, chose Ubald because of forgiveness, wears Robert like a scar, and is always trying, trying, trying.

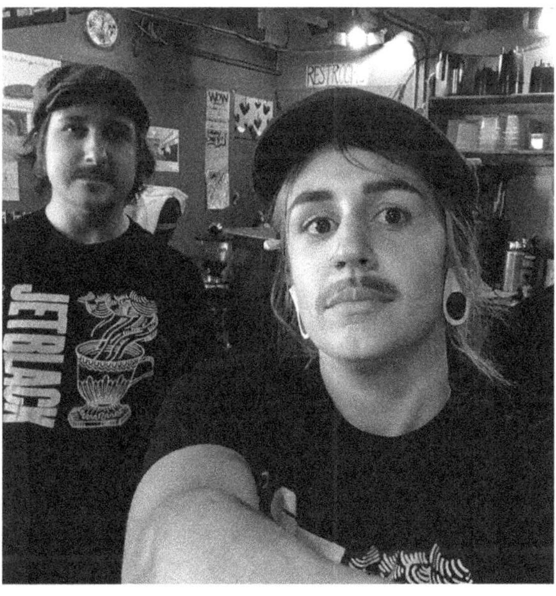

When not disguised as Daniel, **Ellen** enjoys making small work to usher intimacy and the artistic hand, prefers walking places, and will take a coffee at any time of day.

www.ingramcontent.com/pod-product-compliance
Lightning Source LLC
Chambersburg PA
CBHW071506130726
47997CB00006B/2450